PALESTINIANISM

THE NEWEST ATTACK ON PEACE, HUMAN RIGHTS, AND DEMOCRACY

ALAN DERSHOWITZ

Skyhorse Publishing

Alan Dershowitz Books Relating to Israel, Terrorism, and the Laws of War

The Ten Big Anti-Israel Lies: And How to Refute Them with Truth
War Against the Jews: How to End Hamas Barbarism
Defending Israel: The Story of My Relationship with My Most Challenging Client
The Case Against BDS: Why Singling Out Israel for Boycott Is Anti-Semitic and Anti-Peace
The Case Against the Iran Deal: How Can We Now Stop Iran from Getting Nukes?
The Case for Moral Clarity: Israel, Hamas and Gaza
The Case Against Israel's Enemies: Exposing Jimmy Carter and Others Who Stand in the Way of Peace
Pre-emption: A Knife That Cuts Both Ways
The Case for Peace: How the Arab-Israeli Conflict Can Be Resolved
The Case for Israel
Why Terrorism Works: Understanding the Threat, Responding to the Challenge
Chutzpah

Copyright © 2025 by Alan Dershowitz

All Rights Reserved. No part of this book may be reproduced in any manner without the express written consent of the publisher, except in the case of brief excerpts in critical reviews or articles. All inquiries should be addressed to Skyhorse Publishing, 307 West 36th Street, 11th Floor, New York, NY 10018.

Skyhorse Publishing books may be purchased in bulk at special discounts for sales promotion, corporate gifts, fund-raising, or educational purposes. Special editions can also be created to specifications. For details, contact the Special Sales Department, Skyhorse Publishing, 307 West 36th Street, 11th Floor, New York, NY 10018 or info@skyhorsepublishing.com.

Skyhorse® and Skyhorse Publishing® are registered trademarks of Skyhorse Publishing, Inc.®, a Delaware corporation.

Visit our website at www.skyhorsepublishing.com.
Please follow our publisher Tony Lyons on Instagram @tonylyonsisuncertain.

10 9 8 7 6 5 4 3 2 1

Library of Congress Cataloging-in-Publication Data is available on file.

Paperback ISBN: 978-1-5107-8461-1
eBook ISBN: 978-1-5107-8462-8

Cover design by David Ter-Avanesyan

Printed in the United States of America

Contents

Palestinianism   1

A. The Obsessive Focus on Palestinian Rights and Israel's Wrongs   2

B. Indicting Palestinianism in the Court of Public Opinion   6

C. Why Has the Hard-Left Adopted Palestinianism?   7

D. Palestinianism Is Not About the Rights of Palestinians to a State   12

E. The Newest Manifestation of Jew-Hatred: Anti-Meritocracy   21

F. Comparisons to Germany in the 1930s   25

G. The Double Standard Applied Against Israel   29

H. Israel Is Not Guilty of War Crimes or Genocide   32

I. The Role of the Media in Encouraging Civilian Deaths   36

J. The Future of Palestinianism—and of Israel and the Jewish People   41

K. Palestinianism versus Zionism   43

L. Who Are the Palestinianists?   51

M. Gays, Feminists, and Jews for Hamas   61

N.	Palestinian Violence	64
O.	Free Speech and the Single Standard	67
P.	Peace Through Strength and Self-Reliance	69
Q.	The Focus of This Book and a Personal Note	73

Palestinianism[1]

Palestinianism is not only the newest manifestation of anti-Semitism; it also poses grave threats to peace, human rights, and democratic values. Its dangers must be exposed and challenged in the marketplace of ideas. It is the purpose of this book to pose that challenge and to put Palestinianism on trial for the moral crimes of bigotry, incitement to violence, and destroying any prospects for peace.

By "Palestinianism" I do not mean merely supporting a Palestinian state or the rights and well-being of the Palestinian people. Those are entirely reasonable positions to take. I mean only the obsessive focus on the claims of Palestinians and their supporters—<u>to the exclusion</u> or <u>minimization</u> of the claims of other, more deserving, groups. This singular focus on the "rights" of Palestinians is coupled with an equivalent singular focus on the alleged "wrongs" of only one country—Israel, the nation-state of the Jewish people. It is the coupling of these biases that constitutes the new "Palestinianism" that we are now

---

1 Alternate forms of this ideological and political term are Palestinism, Palestine-ism, or Palestine-centrism.

experiencing on university campuses, in international organizations, among hard-left politicians, and in many media.[2]

A. The Obsessive Focus on Palestinian Rights and Israel's Wrongs

The primary reason the far less deserving Palestinian claims have received so much more support than the more deserving claims of other groups can be summarized in two words: "the Jews." It is <u>only</u> because the Palestinians blame their plight on "the Jews" and their nation-state, while others blame the Chinese, the Turks, the Hutus, the Russians, the Iranians, the Ethiopians, and until recently the Syrians for the genocides and massive violations of human rights. The United Nations has condemned the tiny nation of Israel for its actions with regard to the Palestinians more than they have condemned <u>all</u> the nearly two hundred nations of the world combined. If this does not demonstrate an obsessive focus on Palestinianism, anti-Israelism, and anti-Semitism, then nothing does. University students and faculty have rarely if ever protested, encamped against, or boycotted nations or groups other than Israel, even during ongoing mass killings, as in Darfur and Syria. They march only for Palestinians, not for other oppressed national groups, such as the Kurds or Tibetans.

That should come as no surprise. Academic

---

[2] Palestinianism is often accompanied by anti-Americanism because the United States and Israel share so many values and interests.

organizations and departments, mostly in the social sciences and humanities, singled out Israel for condemnation following the massacre and rapes committed by Hamas on October 7, 2023, without mentioning Hamas, hostages, or human shields. Many of these same groups refused to condemn—or even acknowledge—the Hamas murders and rapes; some even justified them as "resistance." This double standard, groupthink propaganda permeates classroom teaching, even in required classes, and influences grades, recommendations, hiring, and promotions. It has turned many university classes into propaganda platforms in which "woke" professors seek to teach students <u>what</u> to think politically instead of <u>how</u> to think critically based on empirical and objective evidence. And it is working, as a recent survey at Yale by the Buckley Institute showed: more students favored divesting from Israel than favored divesting from Iran, China, and Russia. Similar polls showed similar results in other colleges and universities.

If extraterrestrial observers landed on a university campus or at an international organization today, they would conclude that there was only one nation in the world that warranted condemnation for its human rights record. The current demonization of Israel is actually more intense and widespread than it was against Nazi Germany and Stalinism during the depth of their genocidal tyrannies. It may also be no exaggeration to say that Israel has become among the most condemned nations in history—at least in some quarters. This bigotry is both a symptom and consequence of Palestinianism—and its corollary: perverse anti-Israelism!

This obsessive focus on Israel's treatment of the Palestinians cannot be explained by the comparative merits of the Palestinian cause over others, by the comparative suffering of the Palestinians over other groups, or by any other objective or neutral factors. It can only be explained by the fact that the alleged oppressor of the Palestinians is the nation-state of the Jewish people. This obvious double standard against the only Jewish state is a clear manifestation of anti-Semitism and Jew-hatred. Israel is "the Jew" among nations, and those who single it out for unique condemnation are the modern-day anti-Semites and Jew-haters. "Palestinianism"—the obsessive focus on the "rights" of Palestinians and the "wrongs" of Israel—is the newest manifestation of the world's oldest prejudice. And it is getting worse.

It is no excuse to point out that many who self-identify as Jews are among the new anti-Semites. Historically, some "Jews" have led the campaigns against other Jews. Would anyone deny that Stalin's mass murder of Jews amounted to anti-Semitism, despite the involvement of many communists of Jewish origin in the anti-Semitic pogroms? Hitler used Jewish Kapos and Judenrat leaders to implement the Nazi genocide. Palestinianism as well uses hard-left Jews—some simply "useful idiots," others bigoted self-haters—as part of its campaign against Israel and its supporters. Today's most visible manifestation of this perverse use of Jews to condemn Jews is the radical anti-Israel organization called "Jewish Voice for Peace," which is Jewish in name only and opposes Israel's existence as the nation-state of the Jewish people, while supporting groups that kill Jews. One of its most prominent spokespersons, the socialist character author Wallace Shawn, has said that Israel's self-defense actions in Gaza are "worse" than the Nazi genocide against six million Jews, because "Hitler had the decency to try to keep it secret," whereas the Israelis "kind of boast about it." And yes, this ignorant bigot is Jewish.

It is understandable that some Israelis who legitimately oppose their nation's policies toward Palestinians would focus primarily, or even exclusively, on their own government's shortcomings. Likewise, it is understandable that Palestinians prioritize their own concerns over others. But when American Presbyterians, the Vatican, the United Nations, universities, the ICC, New Zealanders, Irish Leftists, South Africans, Quakers, gay leaders, Jewish and Christian actors, and other non-Israelis and non-Palestinians, obsess <u>only</u> about the Palestinians and Israel, <u>that</u> is "Palestinianism," and that is the newest manifestation of what has come to be "acceptable" anti-Semitism and anti-Judaism.

It is in that respect that Palestinianist anti-Zionism has become largely a cover for the new anti-Semitism. The obsessive focus on Zionism as an allegedly evil form of nationalism, colonialism, or racism—when other pervasive forms of nationalism and national liberation based on ethnicity, religion, language, geography, and other identifications, are praised—is double-standard bigotry. This is especially the case with Palestinian nationalism, a relatively new phenomenon, created in response to Zionism and the establishment of Israel. Those who demonize Zionism as ethno-centric, religiously based, and nationalistic, praise these same characteristics when they are essential components of Palestinian nationalism. This, despite the reality that Zionism explicitly demands equal rights for non-Jewish citizens, while Palestinian nationalism, both in theory and practice, excludes Jews and other non-Muslims and/or Arabs from citizenship and equal rights. And when such double-standard bigotry is directed exclusively against the Jewish national liberation movement and its state—Zionism and Israel—it is anti-Semitism.

B. Indicting Palestinianism in the Court of Public Opinion

Zionism and Israel have been under attack and their supporters have largely been playing defense, seeking to justify the ideology of Zionism and the actions of Israel, especially since October 7, 2023. The time has come, indeed it is overdue, for decent people to take the offensive against the dangers and evils of Palestinianism and to put its defenders—many of whom are entirely ignorant of its destructive ideology and its illegal, immoral, and anti-Semitic actions—on the defensive. This book is designed to do just that: to place Palestinianism on trial in the court of public opinion. Up to now, only Zionism and Israel have been on trial. I have been one of their defense attorneys in the court of public opinion. In this book, I assume the role of public prosecutor seeking a guilty verdict. Let the defendants try to secure an acquittal or hung jury based on real evidence. They will not be able to make their case, because the evidence is so strongly against them. So let the trial begin with indictments against the theory and practices of Palestinianism.

In this short book, I will show that the Palestinian cause is comparatively weak, that their current situation of statelessness is largely the fault of their own leaders, and that it is far less deserving of sympathy than other causes that are ignored or marginalized in comparison to Palestinianism. I will also show how dangerous this new Palestinianism is to important values and why it should be confronted with truth and rejected in the marketplace of ideas. Equally important, I will show how damaging Palestinianism has been to the legitimate interests of the Palestinian people, who have suffered grievously by being used as pawns by those who care little about their welfare. In this respect, my attack on Palestinianism is not an attack on the Palestinian people. It is an attack largely against non-Palestinians who exploit the suffering of innocent Palestinian men, women, and children for their own political and bigoted ends. It is a defense of a peaceful resolution that will benefit both Israelis and Palestinians.

C. Why Has the Hard-Left Adopted Palestinianism?

The obsessive focus on Palestinianism is largely attributable to its adoption as a pet cause of the hard-left.

History clearly shows that this support for Palestinianism and opposition to Israel began when the Soviet Union abruptly switched sides during the Cold War. When the Jews of Palestine fought against Ottoman and then British colonialism, much of the world—including the Soviet Union, the European communists, and the American hard-left—supported Jewish efforts to establish an independent democratic state in those portions of Palestine in which Jews constituted a majority. The Soviet Union quickly recognized Israel's Declaration of Independence in May of 1948. Soviet-controlled Czechoslovakia provided the new Jewish state with arms needed to defend itself against the united Arab armies that invaded it. Euro communist parties, the American Communist Party, the National Lawyers Guild, socialist organizations, and other hard-left groups rallied on behalf of the new Jewish state and against the Arab and Muslim theocratic tyrannies and groups that opposed its existence and sought to destroy it. The singing of Israeli folk songs—such as Hava Nagila, Hevenu Shalom Aleichem, and Tzena—was a routine part of leftist gatherings. Left-wing students from around the world—from Berkeley to Scandanavia to London—volunteered to work in kibbutzim.

Israel was the model socialist democracy, defending freedom against the theocratic, sexist, repressive, oil-rich Arab regimes that were largely the product of European colonialism following World War I, when the winning nations divided up the Middle East into spheres of influence. Great Britain was given the mandate over what was then known as Palestine—named by the Romans to de-Judaize the areas then known as Judea and Samaria (Yehuda and Shomron)—which included today's Israel, the West Bank, and Transjordan. The mandate was then divided, with the largest portion given to the newly created nation of Jordan, whose population was mostly Palestinian, but whose ruler—chosen by Great Britain—was a Saudi Arabian ally of Britain named Abdullah, who was subsequently assassinated by a Palestinian nationalist.

The Jewish residents of Jerusalem, Tel Aviv, Tzvat, Haifa, Tiberius, Hebron, and other areas, most of which had Jewish majorities for many generations, rebelled against this European colonialism and sought independence. The left supported this anti-colonialism, anti-imperialism, and anti-theocratism. All that changed on a dime when the Soviet Union switched allegiances and began to support Egypt, Syria, and pan-Arabism. They had oil and geography and a canal. Israel had oranges, sand, and democracy. Suddenly Israel—which remained a socialist state under the leadership of David Ben Gurion's Labor Party—became a pariah. Arab dictatorships and Islamic theocracies that discriminated against women, Christians, and gays became allies of the Soviet Union and those left-wing groups and "fellow travelers" that followed its agendas lockstep. Organizations like the National Lawyers Guild became the legal arm of Palestinian terrorist groups despite its largely Jewish left-wing membership. Palestinianism—though not by that name because the Arabs, in what the Romans denominated "Palestine," did not yet consider themselves "Palestinians"—was gestating. So was the anti-Zionism and anti-Semitism that were critical components of the Soviet shift away from Israel.

In shifting away from Israel, the Soviets were not seeking to bring peace to the region. It must be remembered that every major war between Israel and its numerous Arab and Muslim enemies has been started by Israel's enemies, often with the support of the Soviet Union.[3] Israel's wars have been defensive, made necessary by military aggression and terrorism. This was both before and since the shift.

Beginning in 1948, all the surrounding Arab armies attacked Israel the moment it declared its independence, pursuant to United Nations resolutions, which would have given the Arabs of Palestine a large state. Israel's enemies attacked civilian targets. Israel responded and defeated the combined enemy armies. Palestinianism calls this the "Nakba," suggesting somehow that the disaster was inflicted on Palestinians by Israel. The truth is the Nakba was caused by the attacking Arab armies who wanted to destroy the new nation-state of the Jewish people. The resulting war, in which one percent of the population of the new Jewish state—many of them Holocaust survivors—was killed, resulted in both Arabs and Jews becoming refugees, in similar numbers. Approximately 700,000 Arabs left Israel and approximately 700,000 Jews left Arab

---

[3] The causes of the Sinai campaign, involving France and England, were complex but they include the arming of Egypt by the Soviets.

Palestinianism

countries.[4] Israel absorbed their Jewish refugees. The Arab countries placed theirs in refugee camps that still serve as incubators for terrorism.

The 1967 war began when Egypt—encouraged by the Soviet Union—blocked the Gulf of Aqaba to Jewish shipping in violation of international law, massed its armies illegally in the Sinai desert, and threatened a genocidal war by other Arab nations, especially Syria and Jordan. Israel responded to these acts of war by destroying the Egyptian and Syrian air forces, with very few civilian casualties. Jordan then attacked Israel and was also defeated. As a result of these wars, started by Israel's enemies, Israel captured the West Bank and the Gaza Strip. It then offered to return them in exchange for peace, but all the Arab countries gathered in Khartoum and issued their three infamous noes: no peace; no negotiation; no recognition.

Then came the Yom Kippur War in which Egypt and Syria attacked Israel in an unprovoked attempt to destroy it. Israel won a costly war with many casualties and allowed the Egyptian army to surrender rather than be destroyed.

Since that time (and before[5]) there have been repeated terrorist attacks against Israeli elementary schools, pizza parlors, buses, and other civilian targets. Most recently,

---

4 Both groups of refugees included some who left voluntarily and some who were forced out. Had the Arab armies not attacked Israel, there would have been no "Nakba."

5 Haj Al Husseini incited religious pogroms and terrorism against innocent Jews at prayer twenty years before Israel was established. His goal was to cleanse the region of all Jews.

Hamas violated an existing cease-fire by crossing into Israel and murdering 1,200 innocent people and kidnapping 250. Hezbollah broke a cease-fire and sent rockets into Israel. The Houthis, an Iranian proxy in Yemen, launched unprovoked rocket attacks against Tel Aviv and other civilian areas.

All these attacks were done in the name of Palestinianism, even though some were committed before the term itself had been coined. So those who regard Israel as somehow an aggressor and Palestinians the "victims" must do what so few students and faculty seem ready to do: they must learn the facts, the truth, and the history. If they do, they will see that Palestinianism has been a central cause of war, terrorism, pogroms, and other evils.

D. Palestinianism Is Not About the Rights of Palestinians to a State

Palestinian statehood did not become part of the mix until well after Israel's independence. The leaders of the local Arab population, especially its official head, the Grand Mufti of Jerusalem, who was a close ally of Adolf Hitler, opposed Palestinian statehood. He viewed the Arabs of Palestine not as a separate people, but as part of the greater Arab nation—as "Southern Syrians." He just wanted there <u>not to be</u> a Jewish state in what he regarded as "sacred waqf land." Under Sharia law, land that was once under Muslim control cannot be ceded to another religious group, even if the group constitutes a majority in that land.

This has remained the position of most Palestinian

leaders, including Yasser Arafat, since that time. As former President Bill Clinton put it in October 2024:

> The only time Yasser Arafat didn't tell me the truth was when he promised he was going to accept the peace deal that we had worked out. Which would have given the Palestinians a state in 96 percent of the West Bank and 4 percent of Israel, and they got to choose where the 4 percent of Israel was. So they would have the effect of the same land of all the West Bank. They would have a capital in East Jerusalem. . . . All this was offered including . . . a capital in East Jerusalem and two of the four quadrants of the old city of Jerusalem confirmed by the Israeli Prime Minister Ehud Barak and his cabinet, and they said no, and I think part of it is that Hamas did not care about a Homeland for the Palestinians. They wanted to kill Israelis and make Israel uninhabitable.

Clinton's apt description of the reality on the ground can be summarized in a simple phrase: While Israel seeks to <u>preserve</u> its state, the new Palestinianism seeks to <u>destroy</u> that state.

On December 16, 2024, President Clinton once again, and in quite categorical terms, blamed the Palestinian leaders for why there is no Palestinian state. "When you walk away from a deal like that, you can't come back in twenty years and say you want it now." What Clinton did not mention is that Palestinian leaders had walked away from proposals that would have given them an even larger state in 1938 (Peel Commission), 1947–8 (UN division), 1967 (Security Council resolution), and 2007 (Olmert offer). He also did not say that Arafat's rejection of the Clinton-Barak proposal of 2000–2001 did not come with a simple "no." It took the form of a violent intifada, featuring the blowing up of civilian buses, pizza parlors, and rest stops, during which thousands of Israelis and Palestinians were killed.

Contrast the Palestinian demand for statehood with the claim of the Kurds: the latter have never been offered a state, despite the Treaty of Sevres in 1920 that mandated an independent Kurdish state in what it is now Turkey. Moreover, the Kurds, as distinguished from Palestinian leaders, never sought to end the existence of any other state. Finally, there are many more stateless Kurds than Palestinians, and the Kurds have a language, culture, and ethnicity distinct from their neighbors, whereas—as Haj Al Husseini acknowledged—the Arabs of Palestine are little or no different than the Arabs of Syria, Jordan, Egypt, and other adjoining areas. Indeed, many who today call themselves "Palestinians" have not-so-distant roots in these countries, having moved to the Gaza Strip and the West Bank during the last century and a half from Egypt, Syria, Jordan, and other Arab countries. Finally, the Palestinians have employed violence and terrorism—far more than the Kurds—as their primary means of achieving statehood. Yet no university protesters or international

Palestinianism

bodies call for Kurdish independence, despite their far more compelling—legally, morally, and historically—claim to statehood. Why the difference? Why the double standard? Why are the Palestinians more entitled, more privileged than the Kurds? Why do so many support a group that has, since its creation, rejected the two-state solution repeatedly offered them? The answer is as obvious as it is bigoted: only because the perceived oppressor of the Palestinians is Israel, whereas the perceived oppressors of the Kurds are Turkey, Iraq, Syria, and Iran.

Palestinianism is largely motivated by anti-Israel bigotry, not by considerations that help Palestinians. Even now, supporters of Palestinianism, Palestinian leaders, and Israel haters on the hard-left, reject a two-state solution that ensures that both Palestinians and Israelis can live in safety. This is a reprise of those Palestinian leaders who, even before Israel declared independence, wanted there not to be a Jewish state, more than they wanted there to be a Palestinian state. Palestinianism does not support a two-state solution that includes a nation-state for the Jewish people. The anti-Israel protests in support of Palestinianism did not call for two states. They call for the end of the Jewish state. Most media insist on labeling anti-Israel protesters as "pro-Palestinian." That mischaracterizes them. They are anti-Israel. They, like the terrorists they support, want, in the words of Bill Clinton, "to kill Israelis and make Israel uninhabitable."

Palestinianism does not help the Palestinian people. It is fair to say that over the years, Israel has done more to help the residents of Gaza than has Hamas or the supporters of Palestinianism. Israel has long been the primary supporter of the Palestinian people, both on the West Bank and in the Gaza Strip. Israelis have opened their borders to Palestinian workers, to whom they pay high wages. They have accepted Palestinian patients, including even terrorists, into their excellent hospitals. Some of the Israeli kibbutz residents who helped Gazans were murdered by them on October 7. Even during the current Gaza war, Israel has provided more food, medicine, and humanitarian aid to Palestinians than any country has ever done in comparable wars.

What have other countries that support Palestinianism done to help today's Palestinians in Gaza? Nothing concrete. Norway, Ireland, and Spain, on May 28, "formally recognized a Palestinian state." New Zealanders have protested. South Africa has filed a lawsuit in the ICC. Canada has threatened to arrest Israeli leaders. How does any of that help the Palestinian people? It doesn't. Indeed, it hurts them by raising unrealistic expectations. The only way a Palestinian state will exist is through hard compromises and the difficult direct negotiations to which the Palestinian leadership agreed in the 1993–1995 Oslo Accords.

Consider the fact that no Arab or Muslim nation has been willing to accept Palestinian refugees from Gaza. Perhaps these nations recall that anyone who has tried to help the Palestinians has lived to regret it. When Jordan took them in, the Palestinian leadership tried to overthrow the government of King Hussein in 1970. The attempted coup, known as Black September, ended with the Palestinians being expelled to Lebanon. Once there, a civil war erupted between the Muslims, backed by the PLO, and the Christians, resulting in the PLO being expelled once again, this time to Tunisia in 1982. After Kuwait offered roughly 400,000 Palestinians visas and jobs, and Iraq invaded Kuwait in 1990, the PLO sided with Iraq. After the liberation of Kuwait, an estimated 200,000 were expelled and another 200,000 were not allowed back. In a recent debate on the Piers Morgan show about President Trump's proposal to have Jordan and other Arab states offer to accept Palestinians from Gaza, Mustafa Barghouti, General Secretary of the Palestinian National Initiative, said that if Jordan were to accept most Palestinians, Jordan would cease to exist, presumably because Palestinians would take over the country.

The truth is that few outside of Israel really care about the plight of the Palestinian people. The demonstrations on college campuses which purport to be "pro-Palestine" are far more about condemning Israel than about helping the Palestinians. We never see signs calling for a two-state solution because most of these demonstrators do not want Israel to exist. If a Palestinian state were to be substituted for Israel, it would be a tyrannical regime. The conflict would be between those who want to see it more like Iran, a theocracy that murders dissidents, or more like China, a communist tyranny that also murders dissidents. As long as Hamas remains a viable military and political force, there is no prospect for a democratic Palestine or a two-state solution.

Those who really want to help Palestinians should be supporting Israel's efforts to have Hamas stop terrorizing its neighbor. They should join the United States in demanding that Hamas no longer rule Gaza. That might end the bloodshed in Gaza and start a process which might ultimately culminate in a disarmed Palestinian state that recognizes Israel as the nation-state of the Jewish people.

So let us stop all the virtue-signaling about Palestine and Palestinians and urge the international community, and especially the Arab and Muslim world, to do something to help Palestinian families. That help can come in the form of education, healthcare, employment opportunities, acceptance of refugees, and other humanitarian actions. Gaza could be rebuilt, disarmed, and de-radicalized.

It is not the sole responsibility of Israel to make life better for the Palestinians. Israel withdrew all its soldiers and expelled all its civilians from Gaza in 2005, and it was up to the Gazans to make life better for themselves. But instead, Hamas took over and turned Gaza into a military base with an underground tunnel system and above-ground rocket launchers. Palestinianists call Gaza an "open air prison," without adding that their jailers are Hamas, Islamic Jihad, and other terrorist groups.

In 2000, 2001, and again in 2007, Israel offered the Palestinian leadership nearly all of the West Bank and all of Gaza in a move toward the creation of a demilitarized Palestinian state, but the Palestinian leadership refused to

Palestinianism

accept these opportunities, without even a counteroffer. As an Israeli scholar once put it, "Palestinian leadership does not know how to take yes for an answer."

Those who claim to support Palestinians ought to put up or shut up. Instead of constantly attacking Israel for its imperfections, they ought to be urging Arab and Muslim nations to help the Palestinians in material ways. These would include demanding the end of incitement to violence and the end of the Palestinians' murder-for-hire "pay-for-slay" program, which incentivizes terrorism by paying the terrorists' families for life if they murder Jews.

Those who really want to help the Palestinian people need to place strict conditions on their funding and demand accountability on how their money is spent. Those who claim to support the Palestinians should insist on revising their textbooks, as Saudi Arabia is now doing, and should establish institutions of democracy.

Before a Palestinian state is "recognized," it is crucial to guide the Palestinians out of a society of fear and into a society of freedom, a government that would include freedom of speech and of the press, equal justice under law, property rights, human rights, and, above all, preparing the Palestinians for peace.

Until that is done, all the Palestinian people will get are hollow demonstrations on university campuses, empty recognitions from anti-Israel governments, irrelevant United Nations resolutions, and bigoted demonization of Israel. None of this helps the Palestinian people. It only encourages more hatred, more terrorism, and more war. This is what Palestinianism accomplishes. Nothing more!

The mantra of Palestinianism, chanted at every anti-Israel demonstration, is "Palestine will be free from the river to the sea." This demand has little to do with the rights of Palestinian people; it requires the end of Israel and insists that the entire area between the Mediterranean and the Jordan be "free" of Jews—*judenrein*. Were a Palestinian state to replace Israel in that area, the Palestinian people would be anything but free. They would be controlled by Hamas and other Islamic theocratic tyrannies, in the way the Gaza Strip was controlled when it was "free" between 2005 and October 2023. Dissenters were thrown off roofs, non-Muslims were discriminated against, and gays were murdered. There was one "election" in nearly two decades. Palestinians living in Israel or even on the West Bank were far freer than those living in "free" Gaza. The same would be true if Palestine were to be "free" from "the river to the sea." Palestinians would be free only of Jews, not of the oppression of its tyrannical leaders. Look at Iran, Gaza, Syria, and other "free" Islamicist states.

Palestinianism is not about rights for the Palestinian people. It is about the end of Israel, a nation in which two million Palestinian citizens have the right to vote, to serve in the Knesset, to protest, to practice or not practice any religion, and to leave if they choose to. And it's about its replacement by a Hamas-controlled theocracy with no rights for people who don't adhere to the religious compulsions and fatwas of its Mullahs. This is what

Palestinianism means by "free" when it demands that "Palestine"—<u>not Palestinians</u>—be free: Palestine must be free <u>of Jews</u> and must be free to <u>deny</u> freedom to its own people. Palestinianism is an entirely negative concept—against the rights of both the Jewish <u>and</u> Palestinian people. As Bill Clinton aptly put it: Hamas leaders care less about "a homeland" for the Palestinian people and more about making Israel "uninhabitable" for the Jewish people. Palestinianism is an unjust cause that should not be supported by decent people who want peace and who want dignity for both the Palestinian and Israeli people. It is the current manifestation of the world's oldest hatred.

E. The Newest Manifestation of Jew-Hatred: Anti-Meritocracy

Throughout history, jew-hatred has manifested itself in forms that fit into the cultural fears and phobias of the time.

During biblical times, the Jews of Egypt were hated for being foreigners with too much influence on the Pharaoh. In Queen Esther's day, Jews were regarded with suspicion as "a certain people" who might rise up against authority. Then they were Christ killers. During the Middle Ages when contagious illnesses were spreading, they were blamed and accused of poisoning the wells. From the mid-nineteenth to the early twentieth century when eugenics were at the center of pseudosciences, Jews were charged with being racially inferior. When Soviet communism sought to internationalize, Jews were accused of being cosmopolitan. Then they were accused of being internationalists and capitalists. In the post-World War II period, when communism was the bogeyman, Jews were accused of being "reds" or fellow travelers. Now that anti-colonialism, wokeness, identity politics, and intersectionality are the vogue, Jews are accused of being colonialistic and imperialistic Zionists and their state as being guilty of Apartheid, genocide, and other evils of the day.

Today's enemy of the voguish identity politics of the woke left is meritocracy. According to the new identity politics, people should be judged not on the merits of their <u>individual</u> accomplishments, but rather by their <u>group</u> affiliations. "Intersectionality"—the current academic ideology that dominates the thinking of the hard-left—divides the world into two groups: the oppressed and the oppressors. Jews and their state are oppressors. Palestinians and their supporters are oppressed. The mechanism through which this alleged disparity is addressed is DEI: diversity, equity, inclusion. But these talismanic words, both in theory and practice, are intended to mean precisely the opposite of how they sound. Diversity, as implemented by DEI bureaucracies, has nothing to do with differing views or ideologies. It only means more members of allegedly oppressed groups—such as African Americans, Hispanics, or Arabs—without regard to whether or not individuals have been oppressed personally. Diversity is measured by numbers and percentages of groups. In practice, this produces <u>less</u> diversity of viewpoints and ideologies, because the last thing DEI bureaucracies want are more members of minority groups who do not reflect the dominant views of that group. They certainly do not want individuals—whether or not in the group—who oppose the group ideology. Diversity, as administered by the bureaucracies, does not include conservatives and those who oppose DEI, intersectionality, wokeness, or race consciousness, as they define it. They do not reach out to individuals who favor individual meritocracy over anti-meritocratic group preferences.

The same is true of the "equity" component of DEI. Equity is precisely the opposite of equality. It rejects equal treatment of <u>individuals</u> in favor of <u>reparations</u> based on group affiliation. Equity regards <u>all</u> African Americans and other favored <u>groups</u> as deserving of <u>group</u> benefits, regardless of individual merit. It treats individuals <u>unequally</u>, depending on their group affiliation.

The worst of the three words that comprise DEI is "inclusion." The bureaucracies themselves acknowledge that certain minority groups are explicitly <u>excluded</u> from the benefits of DEI. These excluded groups are comprised of Jews, Asians, and other minorities, whose members, on the whole, are deemed to be <u>privileged</u>. But even unprivileged members of these groups—from poor, less well-educated families—do not qualify for DEI benefits, exclusively because they are excluded from the alleged inclusivity of DEI.

In light of the Alice-in-Wonderland definitions of these terms—as Humpty Dumpty said, "When I use a word . . . it means just what I choose it to mean"—it should not be surprising that the archenemy of DEI, intersectionality, and wokeness is meritocracy. Judging individuals on the merit and demerits of their personal accomplishments is anathema to the collective groupthink of the group and race-based ideologies and practices of the hard-left.

So how does this reality—and no one can deny it is the reality—affect Palestinianism, anti-Israelism, and anti-Semitism? The answer is directly! There are few groups whose success has been as dependent on meritocracy as the Jews. Many Jews have succeeded despite quotas, discrimination, and bigotry. In a world that has never been entirely free of anti-Jewish bias, the success of individual Jews depends on meritocracy. Jews are the poster children of individual meritocracy. And Israel is the poster child of national meritocracy. No nation with fewer natural resources, surrounded geographically by enemies committed to its destruction, and built of the ashes of a genocide, has been so successful in so short a time. And its successes have been achieved through the merits of its citizens, who turned swamps and deserts into orange groves and technological start-ups. Israel is the nation of meritocracy.

Palestinianism is the opposite of meritocracy. Its successes have been based largely on terrorism, anti-Semitism, and the support of outsiders, such as Russia, Iran, international organizations, hard-left academics, and Jew-haters. They have not earned success by meritocratic means. They have been judged not by what they have done, but by who they are—the enemies of the Jewish nation.

It may be understandable, therefore, that the enemies

of meritocracy oppose Israel and support Palestinianism. And it is not surprising that Palestinianism is the current form that Jew hatred is taking around much of the world, especially at universities, international organizations, and groups that claim to be acting in the name of human rights. As has been documented throughout history, anti-Semitism has adapted its mechanisms to the fears, hatreds, and biases of the age during which it operates. Today, meritocracy is the enemy, and Jews and their state are the current manifestation of that enmity.

F. Comparisons to Germany in the 1930s

Though widespread and increasing, current Jew hatred has not reached past lethal levels that resulted in inquisitions, pogroms, and eventually the holocaust. Perhaps it never will, because of Israel's military and technological strength and its "never again" commitment to protect Jews. But there are striking similarities to what took place in Nazi Germany between Hitler's election and Kristallnacht—in the run-up to the Holocaust.

The Jew-hatred that is plaguing university campuses throughout the world today is most reminiscent of what was taking place on German campuses in the mid-1930s. Today's bigotry is justified as political and ideological anti-Zionism rather than religious and racial anti-Semitism, but there is considerable overlap between the two manifestations of hatred toward Jews and toward their nation-state. If Zionism were not the National Liberation movement of the Jewish people, and if Israel were not the state of the Jewish people, there would be far less hatred directed at that pro-western democracy and its supporters.

Denying the centrality of Jewishness to the current hatred is blinking reality. In Nazi Germany, the Jew hatred was initially justified as opposition to communism, just as the Jew hatred in the Soviet Union was justified by opposition to capitalism and cosmopolitanism. Anti-Semitism has long sought to disguise itself as something more benign and acceptable to the mores of the time. Today it is disguised as anti-Zionism and anti-colonialism, but this mask should be as transparent as the masks of the past. The reality is that the Jews of today may be facing hatred comparable to that faced by the Jews of Germany in the mid-1930s. The signs may not be as obvious as they were back then, and as they became in hindsight, but there are enough of them to warrant deep concern, and to trigger action. We do not want the coming generations to say, as was said about the past, that we missed signs that should have been obvious. So let's go back nearly a century for guidance.

Events beginning in late 1932 provided a warning to German Jews that matters could get much worse for them. The electoral success of the Nazi Party and the appointment of Adolf Hitler as Chancellor was the beginning of the end, not only for German Jewry but for European Jewry.

No reasonable person could have predicted the extent of the harm—namely the genocide of six million European Jews—but many German citizens did worry that things could get much worse. Some—in retrospect, not enough—acted on their concerns and left Germany, at considerable cost, both material and emotional.

Following the Reichstag Fire on February 27, 1933, Hitler assumed dictatorial powers. His first victims were communists, Jews, and the mentally "inferior." There were many more communists than Jews, but they were harder to identify. Boycotts against Jewish establishments began; Jewish students and faculty were discriminated against at universities; Jewish lawyers were limited in who they could represent; anti-Semitism was pervasive in the media.

The first concentration camps were established shortly thereafter but their inmates were largely political prisoners, including but not limited to Jewish communists and political dissenters. Jews were beaten on the street, and their businesses suffered greatly.

Despite systemic manifestations of official Jew-hatred, many Jewish leaders—both inside and outside of Germany—counseled silence or muted responses, hoping that matters would improve and that normalcy would return. But they only got worse, culminating initially in Kristallnacht in 1938, and later on in the death camps. Official race laws were enacted and enforced both before and after Kristallnacht.

Some of the worst manifestations of Jew-hatred occurred among young people, especially German students, both Catholic and Protestant. They harassed their Jewish fellow students, and their harassment was supported by prominent faculty members, including some of the most famous intellectuals in Germany. Many artists, musicians, and other cultural icons supported, or did not oppose, Nazism.

The actions of German students in the early 1930s foretold the much deadlier actions of the Nazis in the late 1930s and early 1940s. Some of the German students who harassed Jewish students in 1933 became leaders of the Nazi movement within the next decade. They participated directly in the genocide. Students at elite universities all over the world tend to become leaders of their nation. Their actions as students thus become predictive of what the nation may become when they graduate and assume power. Students who engage in anti-Semitic actions today may become leaders who do worse tomorrow.

In today's world, the most vocal Jew-haters and harassers are radical students, encouraged by many faculty members and tolerated by testicularly challenged administrators. These students, especially at elite universities, are likely to become leaders over the next decade or so. They will be elected to government positions, dominate the media, work on Wall Street, and become influencers. Are their hateful actions, attitudes, and prejudices against Jews and supporters of Israel likely to become mainstream in the near or middle term? That is one of the important questions that must be addressed. The answer may determine the future of Jews in America and throughout the world. We must be prepared for the possibility of an affirmative answer. We cannot repeat the mistakes of the past by assuming that matters will improve.

The major difference between the 1930s and now

can be summarized in one word: Israel. The existence of a powerful nation-state for the Jewish people provides an excuse for bigoted Jew-hatred disguised as political anti-Zionism, while at the same time it provides some assurance that what occurred in the 1940s—namely the Holocaust—will never be allowed to reoccur. The guarantor of "never again" is not the conscience or goodwill of the masses—remember the silence of "good people" in the 1930s and 1940s. It is the military and technological power of Israel, coupled with the economic and political power of Zionists, both Jewish and Christian.

Israel's strength is a double-edged sword: it foments hatred against the nation-state of the Jewish people, not so much because of what it does, but because of what it is: a highly successful nation consisting primarily of Jews that has succeeded based on meritocracy. It is that very success that protects against a repetition of the genocide perpetrated by the Nazis against the Jews. But it is also that meritocratic success that generates hatred among the enemies of meritocracy.

G. The Double Standard Applied Against Israel

To be sure, not all of the hatred directed against Jewish students on campuses around the world can be attributed to pure Jew-hatred or anti-Semitism. Anti-Zionism—unique hatred directed at the nation-state of the Jewish people—is prevalent among some radical left-wing individuals of Jewish heritage. But this cannot explain or justify why Israel alone among controversial nations is subject to the kind of rabid hatred that is being experienced not only by that country but by its supporters, even its critical supporters. If Israel were not the nation-state of the Jewish people, it would not be the target of so much hatred. Of this there can be absolutely no doubt. Actual genocides are taking place in several parts of the world, most notably the Sudan. Human rights violations are rampant in China, Russia, Iran, Belarus, and too many other countries to name. Apartheid based on religion, gender, sexual orientation, and other invidious factors is the rule rather the exception in Muslim nations. Numerous countries now occupy lands taken from other nations by force as the result of military victories. Just one example is Königsberg, an ancient German city that was captured by Russians in World War II, renamed Kaliningrad, ethnically cleansed of Germans, repopulated by Russians, and "annexed" to the Soviet Union, (now Russia), which is hundreds of miles away. There are numerous other current examples as well. Yet the international community, the academy, the media, and young leftists devote more time to condemning the nation-state of the Jewish people than all the other sinning nations of the world combined.

The double standard applied to Israel and its Jewish supporters is reminiscent of the double standard applied to Jews in the early days of Nazi Germany. Jews were accused of supporting Communism, Capitalism, Socialism, Cosmopolitanism, and every other ism. They were accused of working too hard and being too lazy, condemned of being too religious and too secular, of being too nationalistic and too global. They could do no right, and their enemies could do no wrong. If this sounds familiar, it is because it is being replicated today, especially by the hard-left, and most especially among young people.

Consider Israel's war against Hamas in Gaza. The Israeli government, its leaders and soldiers, have been accused of genocide by various international organizations, student and faculty protesters, and even the pope! This despite the indisputable fact that the ratio of civilians to combatants killed by the IDF is lower than in any comparable conflict in history. Even if only the Hamas figures are relied on—and they are provably exaggerated—the ratio would be no more than two or three civilians killed for every combatant. If the figures excluded civilians who were killed by Hamas and Islamic Jihad misfired rockets, civilians who died from other causes, and "civilians" who allowed their premises to be used to fire rockets at Israel, the actual ratio would be closer to one to one. The typical ratio achieved by western democracies is approximately five or six to one! Yet only Israel is accused of war crimes.

The other widespread complaint against Israel is that the lack of an earlier ceasefire was exclusively Israel's fault. But listen to Antony Blinken in his exit interview as secretary of state on January 4, 2025, in the *New York Times*:

> When they [Hamas] saw Israel under pressure publicly, they pulled back. The other thing that got Hamas to pull back was their belief, their hope that there'd be a wider conflict—that Hezbollah

would attack Israel, that Iran would attack Israel, that other actors would attack Israel, and that Israel would have its hands full and Hamas could continue what it was doing. . . . What we've seen time and again is Hamas not concluding a deal that it should have concluded. But fundamentally, look, one of the things that I found a little astounding throughout is that for all of the understandable criticism of the way Israel has conducted itself in Gaza, you hear virtually nothing from anyone since October 7th about Hamas. Why there hasn't been a unanimous chorus around the world for Hamas to put down its weapons, to give up the hostages, to surrender—I don't know what the answer is to that. Israel on various occasions has offered safe passage to Hamas's leadership and fighters out of Gaza. Where is the world—where is the world in saying, yeah, do that, and this, stop the suffering of people that you've brought on?

H. Israel Is Not Guilty of War Crimes or Genocide

Blinken was then asked whether he has "been presiding over what the world will see as a genocide." His answer was an unequivocal "No. It's not." And he is correct: The laws of war are complex and must be adaptable to different threats. Israel is now battling three terrorist groups: Hezbollah, Hamas, and the Houthis. The United States continues to fight against ISIS and related terrorists in several parts of the world. It is important therefore to

Palestinianism

understand the status of terrorists under the laws of war. Terrorists are not regarded either as civilians or as legitimate combatants.

Under the laws of war, civilians are entitled to certain protections from belligerency. They cannot be explicitly targeted during attacks on combatants, though they may become collateral victims of such legitimate attacks. They may be detained as suspected terrorists, but once their status as civilians is confirmed, they are entitled to due process and other rights.

Legitimate combatants also have certain rights, especially after they are captured. They must be treated as prisoners of war and not as ordinary criminals. They may not be tried as criminals for their legitimate military actions.

What about terrorists? They can be detained without due process and without being treated as prisoners of war. The law is unclear as to their long-term status, but certain factors are beyond dispute. Once they are in captivity, they cannot be tortured or killed, but they can be subject to extensive interrogations and have no right to consult counsel or to contact relatives. They can be held until the belligerency is over, and even then, they can be tried for crimes under the laws of the country holding them.

Most importantly, a terrorist who kills a combatant can be found guilty of murder. That would not be true of a legitimate combatant who killed another combatant in the course of a war. A terrorist does not have the same rights as legitimate combatants, even during a war. After being captured, they need not be given the rights of an ordinary civilian to counsel or due process. They can be tried by court martial or other military procedures. The specifics are determined by the domestic laws of the country holding them, not by international law.

To put it bluntly, a terrorist is an "outlaw" in the literal sense of that term, unprotected by the ordinary rules of international law, because terrorists don't abide by these rules themselves.

The killing of Osama bin Laden illustrates the tactics that can be employed against terrorists, even "retired" ones.

During belligerency, terrorists are appropriate targets regardless of whether they are actually engaged in terrorism at the time of targeting. Thus, the Hezbollah members who were given communication devices by Hezbollah commanders were appropriately blown up by Israel, even while they were engaged in civilian activities. The only issue there was collateral damage: Was the risk to non-terrorists proportionate to the military benefits in killing and disabling terrorists? The answer to that was clearly yes in the context of the use of explosive devices in Lebanon.

In general, the law of war is not crystal clear in regard to terrorists and terrorism. Most of these laws were written, largely by academics, before terrorism became as prominent as it is today and when the distinction between combatants and terrorists was far clearer than it is now. Most terrorists live among civilians and interact with members of their families, friends, and associates. But they continue to engage in terrorism on an ongoing basis.

It would be useful for new laws to be enacted that

clarify the legal status of terrorists. It is doubtful that such laws could be written neutrally and objectively today, because so many academics tend to lean left against Israel, and are more sympathetic to terrorists and terrorism than is the general public.

The "laws" being selectively applied by the International Criminal Court and the International Court of Justice demonstrate the bias of contemporary "courts." In the absence of fair laws, deference should be paid to legitimate armies that are battling illegitimate terrorists. This is especially so with regard to nations like Israel and the United States, which have stringent domestic laws governing the treatment of terrorists.

Targeting of civilians by terrorists has become a primary tool of anti-Israel and anti-American warfare. Yet the rules governing such warfare—especially the vague laws regarding the rights and powers of democracies confronting lawless terrorism—often require such democracies to fight their enemy with "one hand tied behind their back" (to quote an Israeli Supreme Court justice.)

The time has come to clarify the laws of war, to empower democracies to have the upper hand in the growing war against lawless terrorism. If this appropriate balance cannot be achieved by international bodies, then democracies should rely on their own laws to strike the balance in favor of legitimate armies and against illegitimate terrorists.

I. The Role of the Media in Encouraging Civilian Deaths

Following the death of Hamas leader Yahya Sinwar, documentary evidence has emerged confirming what many observers already knew: namely, that Sinwar weaponized the death of Gazan civilians, especially women and children.

He understood that the media would emphasize these civilian deaths, attribute them all to Israel, and increase the pressure on the Israeli government to satisfy Hamas's unreasonable demands. This is how the *Wall Street Journal* put it on June 10, 2024, following a lengthy investigation:

> Arab mediators hastened to speed up talks about a cease-fire. . . . Sinwar in a message urged his comrades in Hamas's political leadership outside Gaza not to make concessions and instead to push for a permanent end to the war. High civilian casualties would create worldwide pressure on Israel, Sinwar said.

This may be the first time in military history that leaders have admitted putting their own people in harm's way to increase the casualty figures. This "dead baby strategy" has been used by Hamas for decades. Their leaders regard increasing the reported number of civilian casualties among Palestinians as necessary to victory, both in the court of public opinion and in the courts of law. Hence, they declare these dead civilians to be martyrs and encourage civilians to remain in dangerous places and among Hamas combatants.

Without the support of the media, this strategy would not succeed. It requires that the media report Hamas-generated civilian casualty figures uncritically and without investigating the underlying components of the reported figures.

So the media report upward of 45,000 dead Palestinians. Although they could easily distinguish between combatant and non-combatant deaths, Hamas refuses to do so. Instead, they distinguish between male adults, women, and those who they describe as "children." They fail to acknowledge that many of these so-called children were also combatants. Hamas lists anyone eighteen or under as a child, regardless of whether they are fifteen, sixteen, seventeen- or eighteen-year-old terrorists who have been recruited and trained by Hamas to murder Israelis. They do the same with women, conveying the impression that only men are terrorists.

Moreover, they fail to distinguish friendly-fire casualties that resulted from rockets fired by Hamas, Islamic Jihad, and other terrorist groups whose rockets have a high failure rate, with many landing in Gaza.

They suggest that all non-Hamas members are innocent civilians. But non-Hamas "civilians" were directly involved in the massacres, rapes, and kidnappings of October 7, 2023. Others cheered on these barbarians as they returned to Gaza with their live and dead hostages. Still others allowed their homes to be used to imprison hostages. Many contributed to Hamas financially and in other ways. Then there are the human shields—some voluntary, some coerced—who died as a result of deliberately being placed in harm's way pursuant to the Sinwar strategy of maximizing civilian deaths.

Accordingly, no one really knows the precise number of completely innocent Palestinians who have been killed. It would not be surprising if a careful breakdown of the dead resulted in a much lower figure for totally innocent Palestinians, whose deaths can reasonably be attributed to Israel, rather than to the Sinwar strategy. Even if Hamas's exaggerated numbers were believed, the figure would be remarkably low in comparison with casualty figures in other urban wars fought by NATO and democratic countries. It would represent an approximate ratio of two or three civilians killed for every combatant killed. And it would mean that a tiny percentage of Gaza's civilian population died in a war started by Hamas and fought behind civilian shields. In comparable urban wars, the ratios have been worse for civilians. This is not "genocide." It is self-defense.

Yet the media make it seem as if Israel is the worst offender in history. And useful ignoramuses on university campuses, along with bigots in international organizations, falsely accuse Israel of genocide, despite the largely successful efforts of the IDF to reduce civilian casualties to the minimum possible, consistent with achieving their military goals.

The time has come for credible investigations and evaluations of the actual numbers of Gazans in the various categories who have been killed. In the absence of an honest accounting, the media will continue to do Sinwar's nefarious work in increasing Palestinian casualties in order to increase the pressure on Israel. The result of implementing the Sinwar strategy, even after his death, will be more Palestinian deaths, continuing warfare, and the demonization of Israel. This is precisely what Sinwar asked his followers to do after his death. He should not be permitted to achieve his murderous goals posthumously. Reporting the truth will prevent that from happening, because the Sinwar strategy relies on mendacious and selective reporting by the media.

Sadly, the media's dangerous cooperation with terrorists tells us more about them than about the war about which they purport to be "reporting."

But these realities—and others by knowledgeable officials—do not satisfy the zealots of Palestinianism, because to them, the facts do not matter. No evidence can exculpate Israel or inculpate Hamas. That is Palestinianism. That is why Israel must disregard the false criticisms and condemnations, regardless of how widespread, and do what is necessary to protect its people while doing its best to publicize the truth.

The other reality is that the world must be open to new ideas about Gaza. A return to the status quo before October 7, 2023, will assure continuing conflict. That must be changed. An analogy to World War II may be relevant. The lead-up to that war involved the presence of three million ethnic Germans in Sudetenland, an area of

Czechoslovakia. Most of these Germans supported Hitler and wanted to become part of the Third Reich. Hitler used this as a justification for demanding that result, which he achieved at the notorious Munich Conference. Many non-Germans were forced to move out of the area that had been home to their ancestors for centuries. Most of the Jewish residents were sent to death camps.

At the end of the war, nearly three million ethnic Germans were expelled with the agreement of the participants of the Potsdam Conference, including Prime Minister Winston Churchill and President Harry Truman. This transfer of population was thought to be necessary to secure an enduring peace in central Europe.

A far larger transfer of populations also occurred when Pakistan was divided from India in 1947.

These transfers and others had enormous consequences—physical, psychological, emotional—for innocent people. But they were largely accepted by the international community on the principle that peace is more important than place. (For other examples, see Andrew Roberts, "The Historical Case for Trump's Riviera," *Washington Free Beacon*, Feb 8, 2025).

Populations have been transferred for reasons less important than peace. Tens of thousands of Egyptian and Sudanese Nubians were relocated to build the Aswan Dam. Other transfers—some temporary, others permanent—have taken place throughout history. Indeed, movements of populations have been a regular part of history from the beginning of the human experience.

Solving the problem of Gaza that has been the cause of so much death, destruction, and suffering will require bold thinking, rather than a return to the untenable status quo that would inevitably maintain Hamas as a dominant force in that enclave. No solution is without considerable human costs and risks. But all reasonable alternatives should be considered and negotiated.

J. The Future of Palestinianism—and of Israel and the Jewish People

No one can know the future with certainty, but trends are discernable and cannot be ignored. One such trend is that everything Jewish—beginning but not ending with the nation-state of the Jewish people—will, in the future, be less subject to meritocratic evaluation and treatment than it was during the past "golden age." Their successes will not be dependent on being <u>selected by others</u>, but rather by their own self-proving accomplishments. To paraphrase Tennessee Williams in *A Streetcar Named Desire*, we will not be able to depend "on the kindness of strangers." We will have to depend more on ourselves. We will have to follow the admonition of the great sage Hillel: "If I am not for myself, who will be for me?" without neglecting his second admonition: "But if I am for myself alone, what am I?"

The quickly changing dynamics with respect to Jews and their nation-state transcends the relatively new development of "Palestinianism." Indeed, Palestinianism may only be a symptom of the newest manifestation of the oldest hatred. Whether it is the "chicken" or the "egg" matters less than that it is a major ingredient in the recipe book of the poisonous brew of anti-Semitism. It must be confronted with the best antidote available in a democracy: truth. And it must be confronted now, before it can no longer be contained, as it could not be during prior eras. That is why Hillel's third admonition may be the most important of all: "If not now, when?"

Let me quote another Jewish sage—Bob Dylan. In his 1983 song, "Neighborhood Bully," which is too rarely played these days, he mocks the singling out and maligning of Israel as the "bully" of the Middle East, despite it being "outnumbered a million to one," having "no place to escape to" and being expected to "lay down and die when his door is kicked in." In addition to mocking the singling out of Israel, Dylan also condemns the lack of sympathy for the Jewish people—though he doesn't explicitly identify them or their state by name: "Driven out of every land, wandered the earth and exiled man, seeing his family scattered, his people wounded and torn, it's always on trial for just being born." Yet they are called "the bully."

Bob Dylan's "Neighborhood Bully"—written more than forty years ago—captures the essence of current-day Palestinianism, anti-Israelism, and anti-Semitism, under which the historic victim of the world's bullying—the Jew—is now regarded as the "bully" because he "lives to survive."

We will survive and thrive if we are not bullied by the biases of Palestinianism and are treated equally, fairly, and without discrimination by the world. The central blessing by and to the Jewish people is Shalom—peace. That is not too much for which to ask.

K. Palestinianism versus Zionism

Both Palestinianism and Zionism purport to be national liberation movements for their people. Both are "isms," which for some is an automatic negative. Perhaps that is because the Palestinian cause declined to add that suffix. Or perhaps because it doesn't want to use the same suffix—Palestinianism—so proudly used by Zionists. Labels aside, there are some conceptual similarities between the two national movements. But there are also enormous differences. Zionism is constructive. Palestinianism is destructive. Zionism sought to create a state. Palestinianism seeks to destroy a state.

The goal of Zionism in its pre-Israel form, advocated by Theodor Herzl, David Ben-Gurion, Chaim Weizmann, and other early Zionists, was to create a state for the Jewish people who were being oppressed, discriminated against, and during the Holocaust, subject to genocide. No country would admit the Jews who sought to escape from Nazism. Even the British mandate of Palestine was closed to Jews in the run-up to and during the Holocaust. It was only natural therefore that as soon as the new state of Israel was established, it opened its doors to every Jew, welcoming survivors of the Holocaust, Jews who were subject to discrimination as *dimmis* in Muslim states throughout the Middle East, and other Jews throughout the world.

Jews were the aboriginal population of what was named Palestine by the Romans in an effort to de-Judaize it. Most of the Jews who established a Jewish state in what had previously been called Judea, were descendants of Jews who had been forced out of Judea by the Romans, the crusaders, and other colonist usurpers. They were not like the British colonists who took over New Zealand, Australia, Canada, and the United States. These colonists had no historic roots in the land they permanently occupied, displacing much of the indigenous population.

Zionism was different. It sought to have Jewish people, who had been living as second-class (at best) "guests" in other people's nations, return and establish a small nation on land that had never been an independent and separate nation since the Romans destroyed Judea. Zionists purchased land from Syrian distant landowners and built kibbutzim and towns in which they were the majority population.

As early as 1922, Winston Churchill recognized that the Jews of Palestine already had "national" characteristics and were well on their way to building a Jewish homeland:

> During the last two or three generations, the Jews have recreated in Palestine a community, now numbering 80,000 of whom about one-fourth are farmers or workers upon the land. This community has its own political organs: an elected assembly for the direction of its domestic concerns; elected councils in the towns; and an organization

for the control of its schools. It has its elected Chief Rabbinate and Rabbinical Council for the direction of religious affairs. Its business is conducted in Hebrew as a vernacular language, and a Hebrew press serves its need. It has its distinctive intellectual life and displays considerable economic activity. This community, then, with its town and country population, its political, religious and social organizations, its own language, its own customs, its own life, has in fact "national" characteristics. When it is asked what it is meant by the development of the Jewish National Home in Palestine, it may be answered that it is not the imposition of a Jewish nationality upon the inhabitants of Palestine as a whole, but the further development of the existing Jewish community, with the assistance of Jews in other parts of the world, in order that it may become a center in which the Jewish people as a whole may take, on grounds of religion and race, an interest and pride. But in order that this community should have the best prospect of free development and provide a full opportunity for the Jewish people to display its capacities, it is essential that it should know it is in Palestine as of right and not on sufferance. That is the reason why it is necessary that the existence of a Jewish National Home in Palestine should be internationally guaranteed, and that it should be formally recognized to rest upon ancient historic connection.

That is not colonialism. It is nation building.

Until Israel was established in 1948 and immediately attacked by all the surrounding Arab armies, Zionists did not capture land by force. The land they acquired was obtained peacefully and legally: by contract, treaty, and other lawful means. Zionism succeeded in building a viable state that has thrived for more than three-quarters of a century. It has contributed more to the world—medically, technologically, literarily, academically, agriculturally, and in many other ways—than any country in history during that time. It turned deserts into arable lands, swamps into orange groves, empty areas into universities and medical centers, and start-ups into businesses that employ thousands of Jews and Arabs. It revived a dead language. It rescued millions of people from the oppressions of the Soviet Union and Muslim tyrannies such as Iran and Syria, and made them equal citizens of the only real democracy in the Middle East. And it would have done even more if Palestinianism—before and after the Arab residents of what became Israel called themselves Palestinians—had not continuously attacked and tried to destroy the nation-state of the Jewish people. Imagine the additional contributions Israel could have made if it did not have to prioritize military defense over civilian scientific achievements. It could have turned its swords into plowshares, its nuclear bombs into nuclear medicine, and its military intelligence into more constructive uses. Yet, despite the need to devote so much resource to self-defense, it has become a world leader in so many areas. That's Zionism.

The Israel built on Zionism is both the Athens and Sparta of the Middle East. In ancient Greece, Athens was known for its philosophers, scientists, and theorists of democracy. Sparta was known for its military prowess, its bravery, and its ability to defend itself against enemies. In today's world, in order to be Sparta, a nation must also be Athens. Wars are no longer merely battles of physical strength. They are conflicts in which intelligence, technology, and science prevail.

It is precisely because Israel is Athens—a world leader in science, technology, and democracy—that it is also Sparta. This has been shown dramatically by Israel's technological superiority over its enemies, as reflected by its targeted attacks on its enemy's leaders and terrorist murderers.

This was illustrated most dramatically by how it turned Hezbollah's communication systems into weapons against the terrorists themselves. It was also demonstrated by its use of sophisticated intelligence to locate and neutralize leaders of Hamas and Hezbollah. Even the killing of Yahya Sinwar, though somewhat fortuitous, was facilitated by a small drone that flew into the house in which he was hiding.

Israel is a tiny country, both in size and population, with few natural resources and with borders that are difficult to defend. Yet since even before its establishment in 1948, it depended on its academic as much as its military prowess to overcome these disadvantages by relying on education, innovation, and planning.

It hasn't always worked, as evidenced by its intelligence failures on October 7, 2023—failures that diminished its deterrence and encouraged adventurism by Iran and its proxies. Over the past year, though, the IDF's deterrence has been restored largely by its technological successes.

Everything would change, however, if Iran were allowed to develop and threaten to deploy a nuclear arsenal. There is no completely certain technological defense to nuclear-tipped ballistic missiles. If even one made it through Israel's excellent defense system—enhanced by America—it could mean the end of Israel.

As Iran's former president warned: "Israel is a one-bomb state." Even one successful nuclear attack on Tel Aviv or Jerusalem would constitute an existential catastrophe for Israel.

Nor can Israel hope to deter such an attack by threatening to retaliate against Tehran with a nuclear attack on that population center. As Prime Minister Menachem Begin said in 1981 after he ordered the preventive destruction of the Iraqi nuclear reactor at Osirak, "Israel will never incinerate millions of innocent children." Being Athens—with its deep commitment to democracy, values, and humanity—has its drawbacks when it comes to deterrence.

There are limits to what a democracy will do—limits that tyrannies do not have—even in response to attacks on its citizens. That is why Begin said Israel must <u>prevent</u> rather than <u>respond</u> to a nuclear attack, as it did in Iraq and Syria, and as it must do with Iran.

Israel, along with America, is currently using technology in an effort to thwart Iran's nuclear ambitions. Yet cyberattacks and targeted assassinations may not be enough. A military attack on Iran's nuclear facilities may be required. Such an attack will make use of Israel's technological and scientific advantages, but in the end, its success may depend as much on the courage of its pilots and other soldiers.

It is the creative combination of Athens and Sparta—technology and bravery—that has allowed Israel to implement the blessing of the Psalmist: "God will give the Jewish people strength," and only then "will they be blessed with peace." Jewish history throughout the ages and Israeli history of the last century have proved beyond any doubt that morality alone will not prevent anti-Semites and anti-Zionists from destroying us.

We had morality on our side during the Holocaust, and we had morality on our side on October 7. The reason we will never again experience a holocaust is not because our morality has improved. It is because the Israeli army is stronger than its enemies and the Jewish people around the world use their strength in the interest of self-preservation.

Zionism, Judaism, and the Jewish people are under attack all over the world, especially from the left and most especially from young people who represent the increasing dangers we face in the future.

The response requires a continuing combination of Athens and Sparta. Israel and the Jewish people must continue to excel at science, technology, education, morality, and democracy.

Israel cannot afford—at least not yet—to turn their swords into plowshares or their nuclear weapons into nuclear medicine. It must use its Athenian attributes to make Israel an even stronger Sparta in order to thwart the destructive goals of Palestinianism.

The central goal of Palestinianism has never been nation building. It has always been nation destruction. What Bill Clinton correctly said about Hamas has generally been <u>true</u> of all Palestinianist groups: "Hamas did not care about a homeland for the Palestinians. They wanted to kill Israelis and make Israel uninhabitable." Their goal was to destruct, not construct. This has been true from the very beginning, when the leader of the Palestinian people, Haj Al-Husseini, told the Peel Commission in 1937 that the Arabs of Palestine did not want a state. They just wanted there not to be a Jewish state. This was true when the Palestinians turned down proposals that would have resulted in a two-state solution in 1938, 1948, 1967, 2000–2001, and 2007. It was true in 2005 when Israel completely ended its occupation of the entire Gaza Strip, which the Palestinians could have turned into a self-governing democracy—a "Singapore on the Mediterranean." Instead, Hamas, with the support of many of the Gaza population, overthrew the Palestinian authority—murdering many of its leaders and functionaries—and established a theocratic tyranny that used its enormous resources, given it by European countries and Israel, to try to destroy Israel by building terror tunnels, rocket launchers, and other offensive weapons designed to "kill Israelis and make Israel uninhabitable."

Their effort culminated in the massacres and rapes of October 7, 2023, that were praised and applauded by most Palestinians and a great many supporters of Palestinianism throughout the world.

That is Palestinianism: destroy, do not build; kill, do not seek peace; feed the war machine, not the people; protest, do not produce; propagandize, do not educate.

The goal of Zionism was to <u>build</u> a state. The goal of Palestinianism is to <u>destroy</u> a state.

In these respects, destructive Palestinianism is the opposite of constructive Zionism. Yet to so many people around the world, who are willfully ignorant of the facts, the history, and the current reality, Palestinianism is "good" and Zionism is "bad." This immoral, ahistorical, and biased inversion distorts reality and makes any realistic peace more difficult.

L. Who Are the Palestinianists?

The next time you see what is called a pro-Palestinian— really an anti-Israel—demonstration or protest, try to identify the participants. Who are these Palestinianists who, by their actions and advocacy, distinguish themselves from reasonable supporters of statehood and human rights for all stateless and oppressed people?

The perpetrators of Palestinianism fall into several overlapping categories and subcategories. The first is comprised of some Palestinians themselves, along with their Arab and Muslim supporters.

Three subgroups comprise this large group. The first are radical religious extremists who believe that Sharia prohibits non-Muslims from having a state or homeland on Waqf (Muslim) land. These uncompromising zealots regard all of Israel as exclusively and permanently Muslim property. They demand an end to Israel and its replacement by an Islamic entity governed by Sharia law. There is no room for negotiation under this view—only conquest by any means. For them it is a zero-sum game. There cannot be a two-state solution, or indeed any solution that leaves Israel standing.

From its very beginning, Palestinianism—under different labels but similar ideologies—has been dominated by this religious fanaticism. The founder and leader of the Arab movement in what became Israel, was Haj Al Husseini, the Grand Mufti of Jerusalem, who spent the Second-World-War years in Berlin with Hitler, who he met with and sought to emulate. Husseini did not try to sugarcoat his anti-Jewish motivations of the Arabs he represented. His hatred of everything Jewish was based on a combination of Islamicist religious bigotry and Hitlerite racist anti-Semitism. Following the German defeat, he was declared a war criminal and escapted to Egypt, where he continued his anti-Israel activities.

Husseini, who is still a hero to most Palestinianists, spoke for his people. They did not want a Palestinian state because they regarded themselves not as "Palestinians," but rather as southern Syrians and part of the greater Arab people. They had two demands: no Jewish state or homeland, regardless of how tiny, and regardless of whether it was on land legally acquired with a significant Jewish majority; and making the area *judenrein* through ethnic cleansing of most of the Jewish population. Any remaining Jews—and there would be few, if any—would be *dimi*, second-class guests, subject to the control of the Muslim clergy. This was and still is the essence of religious Palestinianism. It is central to the charter of Hamas and to the ideology of Hezbollah, both of which are based on Husseini's Palestinianism. It is the dominant view among current Islamicist Palestinianists.

Then there is left-wing political Palestinianism, dominated by communists under the leadership of the Popular Front for the Liberation of Palestine. As is obvious from its name, the immediate goals of this secular, radical ideology are similar to those of the Islamicist Palestinianists but broader. They want to overthrow not only Israel (from the river to the sea) but also the other imperial, colonial, and capitalistic regimes in the entire Middle East and beyond. Their ultimate goal is to overthrow all Western, secular democracies. Including the United States and Europe. They want to replace these "fascist tyrannies" with people's republics like China, North Korea, and Cuba.

The third and by far the least influential group of Palestinians who can be called Palestinianists are represented by the Palestinian Authority in Ramallah and other parts of the West Bank. These more "moderate"

Palestinianists claim to support some version of a two-state solution envisioned by the Oslo Accords in 1993, as well as other compromises.

I have met with leaders of this group on several occasions, and if they spoke on behalf of a majority or even a plurality of the Palestinian people, there might be some cause for optimism, but they don't. Polls show that most Palestinians support Hamas and oppose a two-state compromise. Recall that it was the PA that turned down all previous offers of a Palestinian state on nearly all the West Bank because it would require them to recognize Israel as the legitimate nation-state of the Jewish people. The current president of the Palestinian Authority told me that he could not recognize Israel as a Jewish State or as the State of the Jewish people. Leaders of the PA feared that if they recognized Israel, they would be assassinated, as were previous Arab leaders including Anwar Sadat and the grandfather of the current king of Jordan.

Despite being more moderate than the first two categories of Palestinianists, the Palestinian Authority and its supporters clearly qualify for inclusion in the larger category of Palestinianists, because they focus only on the alleged rights of Palestinians and the alleged wrongs of Israel and Zionism, to the exclusion of all other rights and wrongs.

This may be understandable, if not commendable, because they themselves are Palestinians and they see the world through the narrow and self-serving prism of their own situation. I recall my grandmother's narrow focus: "Is it good or bad for the Jews?" But she didn't purport to be a national and international leader. She was an uneducated woman whose entire world was limited to her Jewish surroundings and the discrimination faced by her fellow Jews.

That cannot be said of the large number of rabid Palestinianists who are not themselves Palestinians, but who obsess only about the alleged rights of the Palestinians and the alleged wrongs of Israel, to the exclusion of all other far more worthy causes. It is this category of extremist Palestinianists to which we now turn.

The protesters, encampers, and chanters who have soiled our campuses since October 7, 2023, consist of a motley crew of Arab and Muslim self-servers, joined by radical anarchists and communists who now hide under the more benign label of "socialists." Many of these disruptive radicals will exploit any cause *du jour*—and Palestinianism is today's popular cause—to destabilize American institutions, regardless of the merits or demerits. This group includes professional organizers and agitators who raise and earn money—from both foreign and domestic sources—for preparing and orchestrating anti-Israel and anti-American demonstrations. Prominent among these disruptors is Code Pink, which is a front for the Chinese Communist Party and which is as anti-American as it is anti-Israel.

Then there are well-intentioned but ill-informed and hypocritical antiwar, human rights, and "useful idiot" fellow travelers who know and care little about the nature of the organizations with whom they march, nor about the hundreds of thousands of innocent babies and other civilians who have been and are being killed in Sudan, Syria, Cuba, and Iran. They limit their concerns to the much smaller number of Gazans who have died, many as result of being used as human shields by Hamas. These misplaced moral priorities can only be explained by willful blindness, bigotry, and perverse groupthink.

These protesters who chant "revolution," "intifada," and "from the river to the sea" are encouraging and rewarding terrorism, just as racists in the south encouraged lynching by burning crosses and chanting "segregation now and forever." I saw this when I was a young civil rights worker. The current protesters would not appreciate comparison to the KKK, but by any objective measure, the comparison is apt.

Some of these useful idiots have no idea what Hamas did on October 7 and what they are implicitly supporting. They have simply been told what to say, what to chant, and they follow their pro-Palestinian pied pipers from the river to the sea without knowing which river or what sea are being referred to.

Useful idiots, though, must be held responsible when they promote the evils of Hamas. There were useful idiots who marched with Hitler's youths in the 1930s and with Castro's revolutionaries in the 1950s.

Those who chant hateful and bigoted slogans should be identified and their names and school affiliations publicized. Potential employers have a right to know whether job applicants support the rape of Jewish women or are willing to march with those who do.

The First Amendment protects the right to say idiotic things, but the marketplace of ideas—which is the foundation of the First Amendment—also requires that speakers be held accountable for the words they speak, especially if they are hateful ones.

Imagine if the shoe were on the other foot. Imagine if a group of white supremacists were to occupy an Ivy League campus demanding the lynching and rapes of African Americans. Would Columbia University tolerate such bigotry in the name of academic freedom? Most of the students and professors who are defending these student bigots are essentially saying "Free speech for me but not for thee." That is not how the First Amendment works.

There must be one standard for all, but no Ivy League university would apply a single standard. They are part of the "intersectionalist" mentality that supports free speech for those favored by the diversity, equity, and inclusion bureaucracy—but that opposes free speech for those who are disfavored.

Universities are supposed to educate our future leaders. They are failing abysmally in that task. And we will pay a heavy price if the current one-sidedness continues to be encouraged by university leaders.

The final category of Palestinianists is comprised of old fashioned anti-Semites, Jew-haters, and bigots across the political religious and ideological spectrum. They have a pathological hatred of Jews and anything Jewish.

They include classic religious haters of the Jewish religion: the Jews killed Jesus! Racial and ideological Jew haters: Jews will not replace us! Crazy paranoids: Jews control the world! Self-hating Jews: Israel is worse than the Nazis. And an assortment of psychopaths and other mentally disturbed Jew haters.

These overlapping one-issue hypocrites gather together, despite their differences, under the rancid umbrella of Palestinianism. They have in common that none in this inclusive grouping of haters seeks a two-state solution. None seek merely to end "occupations" or the war in Gaza. None want Israel to survive as the nation-state of the Jewish people. None support other more meritorious causes. None express opposition to any nation other than Israel and its allies. It is only Palestine and Israel all the time, regardless of the merits and demerits. "Palestinianism über alles!" "Israel unter allesi."

Many advocate violence, either directly or implicitly, by supporting Hamas and its murderous means. Student groups at many elite universities—including Harvard, Yale, Columbia, and CUNY—have come out in support of Hamas at a time when its terrorists have raped, murdered, and kidnapped women, toddlers, the elderly, and other civilians, and have reportedly beheaded babies. The immoral groups that support such atrocities are composed of both students and faculty members. Many of these individuals hide behind their organizations' names and refuse to identify themselves. They do not want to be held accountable in the court of public opinion for their own despicable views.

The open marketplace of ideas, which I support, allows students to hold and express these views, but it also requires transparency so that the rest of us can judge them, hold them accountable, and debate them.

There are, of course, rare occasions where anonymity is essential. For example, during the civil rights period of the 1960s, identifying members of civil rights groups endangered their lives. There is, however, no such fear here. Groups that oppose Hamas have not been known to advocate violence against those who support it. To the contrary, it is pro-Israel advocates who have been threatened with and suffered from violence.

The students who anonymously support Hamas need not be fearful of anything but disdain and criticism. They should be willing to subject themselves to the marketplace of ideas. They should not resort to cowardly hiding behind the names of prominent organizations such as "Amnesty International at Harvard"—one of the groups that said they "hold the Israeli regime entirely responsible for all the massacres and rapes." They should be prepared to defend these immoral views.

Some students who belong to these organizations argue that they do not personally support Hamas's recent barbarities. They are free to say so and to dissociate themselves from the groups they voluntarily joined. Silence in this context is acquiescence. So is hiding behind anonymity.

Fellow students, future employers, and others should be able to judge their friends and potential employees by the views they have expressed. Teachers should not grade students based on their views. That is why anonymous grading is widely employed at universities.

As a university professor for fifty years, I would not grade down a student because she supported Hamas atrocities. Nor would I befriend such a student. Freedom of speech is not freedom from being held accountable for one's speech. It is interesting that most of the counter-petitions protesting Hamas's activities contain the names of students and faculty, but that is far less true of petitions that support Hamas's atrocities. That is understandable because there is no reasonable defense for what Hamas has done. Those who support Hamas should be ashamed and shamed, and those who oppose Hamas should be praised. That, too, is part of the marketplace of ideas.

Today, too many students are judged by their "identity." Identity politics has replaced meritocracy. Being judged by one's support or opposition to Hamas barbarity is more justifiable.

Let the student newspapers, many of which are rabidly anti-Israel, publish the names of all students and faculty members who belong to groups that support and oppose Hamas. Hypothetically, if a club were formed at any of these universities that advocated rape or the lynching of African Americans, the newspapers would most assuredly publish the names of everyone associated with such a despicable group. Why is this different? Rape has become a weapon of war for Hamas, along with lynching, mutilation, mass murder, and kidnapping. Expressing support for these acts, while constitutionally protected, is wrong. The answer to wrong speech isn't censorship; it is right speech and transparency.

So let the names be published. Let the despicable students and faculty members who support Hamas stand up and defend their indefensible views, and let the marketplace of ideas decide who is right and who is wrong.

M. Gays, Feminists, and Jews for Hamas

Among the groups that have supported the rapes, beheadings, burning alive, mass murder, and kidnappings of Jews by the Hamas terrorist organization that rules the Gaza Strip have been some that purport to speak for gays, Jews, feminists, and progressives. If any of these groups were actually to travel to Gaza, they would be murdered by Hamas.

Hamas has no tolerance for gays, Jews, feminists, or progressives. Indeed, among the people beheaded, raped, murdered, and kidnapped were gays, Jews who support Palestinians, feminists, progressives, and non-Jews. None of that matters to Hamas. If you are a Jew or an Israeli or just happen to be in the way, you are a target of their barbarity.

Why do so many people from groups that Hamas seeks to destroy support that racist organization? The answer is clear: These bigots hate Jews and their nation-state. This has nothing to do with support for the Palestinian people, who are horribly oppressed by Hamas.

Let us remember that these shows of support for the terrorist group Hamas began before Israel had even responded to the Hamas barbarity. There were shows of support for what Hamas did to innocent Jews: rapes, beheadings, mass murder, kidnapping, and torture too unspeakable to show. It was the victimization of Jews that stimulated these displays of anti-Semitism. There were few criticisms by Palestinianists of Hamas for what it did. The most ferocious demonization was against Israel for what it is: the nation-state of the Jewish people. Never mind that there are many Arab and Muslim states. As is typical of bullies, victimizing Jews came when Israel was at its weakest and most vulnerable, still grieving the loss of so many innocent civilians.

Among the most hypocritical supporters of Hamas are "Gays for Gaza." Rainbow flags and posters identifying the protesters as gay were rampant at anti-Israel demonstrations calling for the end of that nation. In Gaza, such signs are illegal. Anyone displaying them would be killed, as was Hamas commander Mahmoud Ishtiwi, who was caught having sex with another man, and promptly tortured and killed.

Gay men in Gaza seek asylum in Israel. The city of Tel Aviv is among the most accepting of gays in the world. But none of this matters to the gay bigots: They put their hatred of Jews above their concern for gay Palestinians.

Even worse is the misnamed group Jewish Voice for

Peace. If its Jewish members (many are not Jews, despite its name) sought to protest in Gaza, they would be murdered or kidnapped. Hamas, like the Nazis, does not distinguish between Jews based on their politics, as evidenced by the fact that some of the Jews killed on October 7 were critical of the Israeli government and perhaps even of Zionism. But that did not matter to the rapists and beheaders of Hamas. To them, a Jew is a Jew, regardless of whether they belong to Jewish Voice for Peace or Likud.

Then there are the feminists, progressives, and labor unions that support Hamas brutality and oppose the existence of Israel.

Hamas is among the world's most anti-feminist groups. It subjugates women to the whims of their husbands and fathers, and tolerates, if not encourages, wife-beating and "honor killing" women who supposedly dishonor their families.

Hamas imprisons progressive critics and does not permit independent labor unions. Its members exploit workers and use child laborers and child soldiers. But not a word of criticism from the bigots who are willing to give Hamas a pass on their fascism as long as they murder Jews. If this is not anti-Semitism, I don't know what is.

Yes, Jews, too, can be anti-Semites. So can gays, feminists, progressives, socialists, and others on the hard-left. Hitler was a vegetarian. Some leading Nazis were gay. Gertrude Stein, a Nazi collaborator, was gay and a Jew. Many university students and faculty, not only in Germany but at Harvard, Yale, Georgetown, and other American universities, supported Nazi Germany in the 1930s. Today's Nazis are Hamas. Today's enablers of Nazism are the students and others who support Hamas. History will judge them the way history has judged Nazi collaborators.

N. Palestinian Violence

The chants and signs in support of Hamas are becoming increasingly dangerous. They go well beyond supporting the people in Gaza, or even opposing Israel's right to exist. Some now defend the murders and rapes committed by Hamas and demand even more violence against Israeli citizens. Protesters chant, "We are Hamas," "We love Hamas rockets," "Burn Tel Aviv to the ground," and "10,000 repetitions of October 7th." A leader of the Columbia rioters recently said, "Zionists don't deserve to live" and that he feels "very comfortable calling for these people to die" (though he later apologized).

If Hamas is not defeated in Gaza, it is likely that its terrorism will extend beyond the Middle East. Already Hamas terrorist cells have been identified in several European cities. It is almost certain that Hamas operatives are planning terrorist attacks in the United States as well. It is not a bridge too far to believe that radicals who claim to be Hamas, love their rockets, and call for the death of Israelis and Jews might take the next step and help Hamas operatives engage in terrorism against US targets. This has occurred in the past among supporters of other radical terrorist groups. They could be recruited to help purchase weapons, identify targets, and even plant bombs. Something similar happened in the late 1960s and early 1970s when American supporters of terrorism became terrorists themselves, including students, professors, and university graduates. They planted bombs, tried to blow up army bases and recruitment centers, and murdered police officers and armed guards. For them, as with today's Hamas supporters, "any means possible" justifies their revolutionary ends. Hamas will do the same if given the opportunity in this country. The line between advocacy, incitement, and actual violence is not always an easy one to draw, though the First Amendment demands that we do so. But common sense also demands we be on guard, lest these lines be crossed invisibly or quietly, as terrorists often do. We may not be able to arrest and prosecute people who advocate murder, rape, and rocket attacks, but we surely have the power, under our constitution, to be concerned and to take constitutionally permissible precautions against the possibility that radicals who advocate violence may well engage in it in the not-too-distant future.

During the Vietnam War protests, law-enforcement authorities were caught off guard. They did not believe college-educated protesters from good families would turn into terrorists. But they did, and people died. Some of the terrorists went to prison. Others did not. Some who went to prison for murder, like Kathy Boudin, were actually hired after their release by universities like Columbia to teach students. Others were befriended by the likes of Barack Obama. The terrorists of the late 1960s and early

1970s were glorified by the media—and continue to be so in films and books. We must never glorify terrorists, for starters. Rather, we must do everything in our power to prevent violent and hateful protesters from turning into murderous terrorists. This must all be done consistent with the First Amendment.

We must be prepared for actual violence from those who currently advocate violence. Certainly, our law enforcement and intelligence agencies must remain on alert, monitoring social media channels and, perhaps, looking for links between, say, protesters who commit crimes and known terror groups and individuals. Track funding sources, too. The lights are flashing; connect the dots. Most of those who today support and admire Hamas will not cross the line from advocacy to terrorism, but some likely will. It is difficult, if not impossible, to distinguish the less dangerous from the more dangerous, but we must try, within the constraints of the Constitution. No democracy can ignore the presence of a dangerous "fifth column" aiming to do us harm at the behest of enemies like Hamas. When you watch these agitators call for "Death to America" and praise Hamas rockets, remember: You may be their next target. As the late Elie Wiesel reminded us, "It may start with the Jews, but it rarely ends with Jews."

Palestinianism is premised on a double standard for evaluating both Palestinian rights and Israeli wrongs. It is also based on the assumption that ignorant observers will believe whatever historical and contemporary falsehoods are spread about the causes of Palestinian grievances and a fair and conservative assessment of Israeli measures to defend its population.

O. Free Speech and the Single Standard

Columbia University's president and other college administrators have stated that the chant "From the river to the sea, Palestine will be free" is permissible political speech. On an abstract level, they are correct. It is also permissible for white supremacists to demand all Blacks be sent back to Africa and all Muslims to Saudi Arabia. The First Amendment protects homophobic, sexist, and transphobic speech too. But would any school permit such bigoted chants? Imagine what would happen if a group of white-supremacist students demanded South Africa be returned to white apartheid control: "From the Atlantic to the Indian Ocean, South Africa should be free of BLACKS and returned to WHITE control!" Would any school tolerate such a chant? Would it take action against such racists? Of course it would. The racist diversity, equity, and inclusion bureaucracy and its bigoted brother "intersectionality" would demand it, and the school would comply. So the issue is not one of abstract free speech. It is whether the school applies the same standard to Jews, Blacks, gays, and other minorities. What is permissible to say against Jews and Israel would not be permissible to say against Blacks or gays. That is the reality. Universities, whether public or private, should apply a single standard of free speech, harassment, and tolerance for dissenting views.

As the Supreme Court has held, there's no such thing

as a false idea under the First Amendment. There is also no such thing as a true or good idea that is given preference over false or bad ideas. There must be what I call "a circle of symmetry." And what is outside and inside the circle must be based on neutral principles. Columbia and other universities must decide whether to ban or permit all racist, sexist, homophobic, anti-Semitic, and other offensive speech. They cannot punish anti-Black racism while tolerating anti-Jewish racism, even if the First Amendment protects both. Columbia and other universities must make a decision: apply the First Amendment and permit all forms of bigotry; or design symmetrical neutral rules that protect all groups equally. What is unacceptable is what most universities are doing today: protecting some minorities favored by DEI and intersectionality over Jews and other minorities disfavored by DEI. This double standard cannot be allowed to become the accepted standard, as it has at Columbia, Harvard, and other universities. Jews are explicitly second-class citizens under DEI and intersectionality.

These ideas have been the source of some of the worst anti-Jewish and anti-Israel demonstrations, petitions, and harassment. As long as these bigoted bureaucracies continue to hold sway at universities, corporations, and other institutions, Jews will continue to be the object of discriminatory treatment in speech, admissions, hiring, and other decisions. These bureaucracies must be dismantled, uprooted, and delegitimized if real equality and meritocracy are ever to be restored, as they should be in every institution. But many universities are doubling down on their commitments to these dangerous ideologies. Presidents, professors, and administrators in most schools are too terrified to challenge these powerful bureaucracies. But they must if the future of America's great universities is to be preserved. It remains to be seen whether the current administration's views on these matters will turn things around.

P. Peace Through Strength and Self-Reliance

The Psalms of David promised the Jewish people "oz"—strength. It then advises them that only if they have that strength will they achieve "shalom"—peace. This has been the lesson of history. The Jewish people have never seen peace and security through weakness, division, or cowardice. During the Holocaust, we had no strength—militarily, politically, economically, or through alliances. We could not fight back, with a few brave exceptions which, however, proved futile. The lesson of the Holocaust and the tragedies that preceded it, is that the Jewish people must be stronger—militarily, technologically, economically, and politically—than their enemies—they must also be more courageous. My late friend, Justice Antonin Scalia, used to remind us that in order to be "the land of the free," we must be "the home of the brave."

The Talmud teaches us that prophecy ended with the destruction of the Temple. We cannot know the future. But certain trends are obvious, and we ignore them at our peril. We must always prepare for every worst-case scenario. Among these possible negative scenarios is that in the future, Israel may not be able to count on the kind and degree of American military support it has long received (though it did not receive such direct support during the war of independence and for years thereafter). The *New York Times* columnist Tom Friedman cautioned that Joe Biden may be the last pro-Israel Democrat president, as that party moves more to the left and the Squad increases its influence. Already, many Democrat senators and Congress members have voted against some military aid proposals. Israel must plan for and be prepared to go alone in protecting its citizens from military, diplomatic, and economic attacks. If today's unthinking anti-Israel protesters become tomorrow's unthinking anti-Israel political leaders, Israel may well have to stand alone. It must be prepared for such an eventuality.

Parallel to this change may be an equally important reversal of fortunes for American Jews, as well as for Jews in Canada, Great Britain, France, Argentina, Brazil, and other countries with significant Jewish populations. The dramatic reduction in Jewish student percentages in elite universities—such as Harvard, Yale, and others—may signify a broader change in the manner by which Jews achieve success in the broader world. A look back at history may help to explain this possible change.

In Czarist Russia, the only route to success for Jews was to make it on their own. They could not count on being selected or helped by others, whether the government or other institutions, such as universities, professional societies, or large businesses. So they became musicians, chess players, entrepreneurs, writers, and other self-directed and self-proving innovators.

A similar, if less extreme, dynamic was at work in other countries in which anti-Jewish discrimination was the norm, if less officially enforced. Even in the United States, there were anti-Jewish quotas and barriers in colleges, medical schools, law firms, banks, and other businesses. Accordingly, Jews found other routes to success that did not depend on being selected or approved by others. They invented Hollywood, Tin Pan Alley, investment banks, and other institutions with few or no external barriers.

In my own case, I graduated from the most elite law school in the country, where I finished first in my class, was elected editor in chief of the law journal and was selected to be a Supreme Court law clerk. Yet I was turned down by all thirty-two Wall Street law firms to which I applied. So I became a law professor at Harvard, which had fewer barriers based on religion, and I developed my own individual law practice. I didn't need to be <u>selected</u> by any Wall Street law firm. Twenty-five years later, when my son graduated from the same law school, the Wall Street law firms had stopped discriminating against Jews and he could get hired by any firm to which he applied.

The golden age of Jewish acceptance—and selection—began in the mid 1960s with the civil rights movement. It may now be ending—not because of the conservative Wasps (white Anglo-Saxon Protestants) who imposed the earlier barriers, but because of left-wing, woke intersectionality and DEI bureaucracies that today have oversized influence in admission, hiring, and selection processes throughout the country. Jews are once again being subjected to quotas and other barriers because—as I have noted—they are regarded as "privileged," "white," and otherwise undeserving of equal treatment. Pursuant to the prevalent ideology of "intersectionality," which divides the universe into oppressors or oppressed based on their "identity," Jews are deemed to be the oppressors of Blacks, Muslims, and other oppressed groups. They are not entitled to the benefits of meritocracy, at least as defined by others—because such meritocracy itself is seen to be part of the oppressors' machinery that intersectionality is designed to expose and oppose. The response of the day is DEI—a mechanism that has been interpreted to exclude Jews and other oppressors. The result has been a return to quotas and barriers of yesteryear. The cruel irony is that Jews, uniquely, have been the victims of both right-wing Wasp exclusion and left-wing woke exclusion.

The implications of this reversion of exclusionary practices, is that once again Jews may have to make it largely on their own. They will be advised to choose career paths in which success is not determined by being <u>selected</u> by <u>others</u>, whether these others are admissions deans at elite universities, hiring partners at law firms, corporate recruiters, or other selectors. I predict that even the selection of prizes and awards such as the Nobel—for which Jews have in the past been selected disproportionately to their numbers—will be influenced by DEI trends, especially in areas that are subjective, like peace, literature, and even economics. It remains to be seen what impact the Trump administration's strong opposition to DEI will have in practice.

Q. The Focus of This Book and a Personal Note

In this short book, I explore the sources of contemporary Jew-hatred, Israel demonization, and other threats to Jewish communities around the world. I demonstrate why I believe things are likely to get worse, as they did in Germany during the late 1930s. I do not believe they will culminate in another genocidal holocaust, but I do believe that when these young bigots grow into influential adults, they will increase the hatred against Jews and their nation-state.

I argue that Jews and their state must become more self-reliant, and less dependent on the approval, support, or selection by others.

I also provide what I believe are appropriate responses to this growing threat, especially the exposure of Palestinianism as a threat to peace, truth, democracy, and the single standard of human rights. There is no perfect solution, just as there was none in the 1930s. But we can do more and better than they did because we have learned the dangerous lessons of history and are determined not to repeat them. Silence and acquiescence are not options in the face of these growing threats. We must take both responsive and proactive steps to avoid any risk that the disastrous past will be repeated, even in part.

Most American Jews and supporters of Israel are currently secure, influential, and self-satisfied. So were the Jews in Germany in 1932. That's why so many of them stayed on, at least until Kristallnacht persuaded them that remaining in Germany was not a feasible option. By then it was too late for many. Remember the St. Louis! And the closing of the doors to Palestine! Some managed to escape. Most of those who stayed were murdered in the years to come. Too many American Jewish leaders refused to risk their own comfort and security to fight for their vulnerable brothers and sisters in harm's way throughout Europe. Too few non-Jewish American leaders cared enough about the Jews of Europe to do anything. The results were catastrophic for world Jewry.

We are currently near the beginning, rather than near the end, of what is a considerable threat to the future of Jews and their nation-state. Although we cannot predict the long, middle, or even short-term consequences of this threat, we must take it extremely seriously in order to minimize the resulting damage. This book offers a road map, based both on history and current reality, for addressing these issues now!

In a previous short book, I catalogued some of the major lies that are now prevalent in the campaign against Israel and its founding principle of Zionism.[6] The best answer to falsehoods is not censorship. It is truth. As

---

6 See *The Ten Big Anti-Israel Lies: And How to Refute Them with Truth* (Skyhorse, 2024).

long as the marketplace of ideas is open to all points of view, none should be censored. In a democracy, the people choose which ideas to accept in the free marketplace. Unfortunately, history shows that truth does not always prevail in the marketplace of ideas, but censorship is an unacceptable alternative.

I take my responsibility seriously as someone who has been called an important defender of the Jewish people and the Jewish state. My dear friend, the late Elie Wiesel, overstated it greatly when he said, "If there had been more people like Alan Dershowitz in the 1930s and 1940s, the history of European Jewry might have been different." I don't think that anything a single private individual could have done would have changed the catastrophes visited upon the Jews by Hitler. Roosevelt and Churchill could have done more to save Jews. The leaders of other nations that closed its doors to Jewish refugees could also have saved Jews. The pope could have saved more Jews by condemning Catholics who participated in the genocide. They all failed in their responsibility.

I don't know whether I can have any real influence on the Jewish future, but I will surely use every resource at my disposal to try to have a positive influence going forward. Hence, this book and others I plan to write, along with activities I plan to pursue in the years left to me. I will not be frightened into inaction. Neither should you. We must expose the new Palestinianism and anti-Israelism for the dangers they pose not only to Israel and Jews, but to the entire world. We must introduce the term

"Palestinianism" into the vocabulary of today's dialogue as a word of derision, and we must distinguish it from support for the legitimate goals and interests of the Palestinian people; and we must do so without fear of being falsely accused of being anti-Palestinian, anti-Arab, or anti-Muslim. We must expose the danger of Palestinianism for what it is: An evil return not only to the demonization of Jews and their nation-state, but also a frontal attack on peace, human rights, and truth, as well as the values of democracy and the rule of law.